Penguins

Susanna
Davidson

Illustrated by
Simon Mendez

Reading Consultant: Alison Kelly
Roehampton University

Penguins live in some
of the coldest places
on earth...

...in a world of ice and snow.

But you can also find
penguins on sunny beaches...

African
penguins

and on grassy islands by
clear, blue seas.

Snares
Island
penguins

There are nearly twenty
different kinds of penguins.

Emperor
penguins are
the biggest.

Fairy penguins are
the smallest.

Chinstrap
penguins have
a black stripe
on their chin.

Yellow-eyed penguins
have yellow eyes.

Rockhopper penguins
have a feathery yellow
crest on their heads.

Penguins might come in different sizes, but they are all the same shape.

Big beak

Webbed feet

They have long bodies
covered in feathers, and
stumpy little legs.

Sleek
feathers

Short
neck

Stiff tail

Penguins are a kind of bird.
Most birds can fly...

...but not penguins.

Their wings are too small
for flying.

And their
bodies are too
heavy to get
off the ground.

11

Penguins use their
wings for swimming
instead. Their wings are
known as flippers.

Penguins plop into the
water head-first

and

dive

down

deep.

13

Underwater, hungry
penguins hunt for food.

They dart after fish, and
sea creatures called krill.

14

A penguin snaps up some
krill in its sharp, pointy beak.

He swallows it whole, in
one big GULP!

Every now and then,
penguins have to pop up
for air.

To get out of the water, a penguin heads for the surface at full speed, then...

Weeeeeeeee!

Once a year, penguins
leave the sea.

They travel across land to
the place where they were born.

Penguins can't walk fast.
They waddle along on their
webbed feet.

Penguins on ice sometimes
flop onto their tummies and
push with their feet.

When they arrive, the penguins gather in huge groups called rookeries.

These stretch as far as the
eye can see.

Rookeries are very noisy
places. All the penguins are
trying to find a partner.

The male and female
penguins call to each other.

African penguins bray like donkeys. King penguins make trumpeting noises.

Penguins bow and flap their flippers too.

They all get into penguin
pairs. Then the female
penguin lays an egg.

Inside the egg, a baby penguin starts to grow. The baby penguin is called a chick.

At first, the chick is just a red blob.

After ten days or so, it starts to take shape.

By the time it is ready to come out, the chick fills the egg.

Eggs must be kept warm,
so the chicks inside can grow.
Most penguins
build nests
and sit on
their eggs.

Other penguins dig
burrows.

But some penguins just balance the egg on their feet.

They cover
the egg with
a flap of skin
to keep it snug.

Peep! Peep!

At last, the penguin chick
is ready to come out. It pecks
a hole in the egg.

30

It pecks and pecks until the top of the egg comes off. Finally, the chick climbs out.

At first, penguin chicks only have fluffy feathers. They can't swim or feed themselves.

Penguin parents go to the
sea to find food. In cold
weather, chicks huddle
together to keep warm.

The chicks can't eat whole food yet. So penguin parents swallow down their food...

...then bring it back up as a thick paste and feed it to their chicks.

When a chick is a few months old, it starts to grow shiny new feathers.

6 months old

4 months old

The old feathers fall off in patches. It is a scruffy time for penguins.

6½ months old

7 months old

Then the chicks waddle
to the sea for the
first time.

They plop
into the water
and dive down deep.

38

They chase fish and catch some in their sharp beaks.

They're ready to take care of themselves.

For the next few years, the young penguins live far out at sea.

But one day, when they are old enough, they return to the rookery where they were born.

There, they get into pairs and
have a chick of their own.

Penguin facts

Gentoo penguins are the fastest swimmers.

Penguins usually live between 15-20 years.

Small penguin eggs only take 28 days to hatch. Emperor penguins' eggs take the longest – 66 days.

Penguins sometimes surf through waves to get onto land.

Penguin words

Here are some of the words in the book you might not know.

 krill - small, shrimp-like creatures that float in the ocean in huge numbers

 nest - a small space used by birds to look after their eggs and young

 rookery - the area where penguins go to lay eggs and bring up their young

 webbed feet - feet that have skin stretched between the toes

Penguin quiz

How much do you know about penguins? Find out with this quiz. The answers are on page 46.

1. Which is the biggest kind of penguin?

2. Can penguins fly?

3. What do penguins eat?

4. What are baby penguins called?

5. How do penguin parents feed their young?

6. Can you name the different parts of this penguin?

A.

B.

C.

D.

Answers to penguin quiz

1. Emperor penguins are the biggest.
2. No, penguins can't fly.
3. Penguins eat fish and krill.
4. Baby penguins are called chicks.
5. Penguin parents swallow down their food and bring it back up as a paste to feed to their chicks.
6.

A. Beak

B. Flipper

C. Feet

D. Tail

Index

Penguin websites

You can find out more about penguins by going to the Usborne Quicklinks Website at www.usborne-quicklinks.com and typing in the keywords "first reading penguins". Then click on the link for the website you want to visit.

Series editor: Lesley Sims. Designed by Abigail Brown.
Consultant: Dr. Finlo Cottier,
Scottish Association for Marine Science

First published in 2007 by Usborne Publishing Ltd., Usborne House,
83-85 Saffron Hill, London EC1N 8RT, England. www.usborne.com
Copyright © 2007 Usborne Publishing Ltd.